Pain

Is

The

Name

Of

The

Game

Nashya M. Williams

Pain Is The Name of The Game

Nashya M. Williams

Copyright © 2018 by Nashya M. Williams.

All rights reserved.

No part of this original work may be reproduced in any way without permission from the author, except by a reviewer. For interviews or any inquiries pertaining to the content of this publication, please contact the author and/or publisher.

Email: Nashya.Williams14@gmail.com

Facebook.com/NashyaMWilliams

Instagram: @Nashya_M_Williams

Edited, Formatted, and Published via *iWrite4orU*: www.iWrite4orU.com

Cover Image

Illustrated by: Jayla Wallace

Designed by: Exonyx Designs

Formatted by: iWrite4orU

ISBN: 978-0-9998842-4-9

Printed in the United States of America

Pain Is The Name of The Game

Pain Is The Name of The Game

"This is Pain"

Muted…………………………………………9
The Silent Killer……………………………..13
Misunderstood………………………………15
Pulsating Headaches………………………...19
Therapy……………………………………...23
Dear Best Friend……………………………27
Backstabber…………………………………31
Lack of Support……………………………..33
Black and White…………………………….35
Missing You………………………………...39
Pain Is The Name of The Game…………….43

Love Is Unfair

"Relationships"

Lust Is Love, Love Is Lust………………...47
In Between The Sheets……………………49
Intimidation………………………………..53
Loyalty……………………………………..55
The Game Has Changed…………………..59
I Apologize………………………………...63
Love Yourself……………………………...69
A Hard Pill to Swallow……………………75
A Change of Heart………………………...79

The Process of Healing

"Healing the Pain"

To Be Free..83
A Mother's Love....................................85
Jeremiah's Ballad..................................87
Authentic...91

Acknowledgments.................................93

About the Author...................................95

Nashya M. Williams

Pain

Is

The

Name

Of

The

Game

"This is Pain"

Pain Is The Name of The Game

Nashya M. Williams

Muted

A young black girl with no voice,
No opinion, no ideas,
Nothing seems to matter
She has been created to cook, clean, serve,
And to be degraded
By the people of her own kind
She has been captured by deceit,
Lies, and broken promises
She screams:
*Can't you see how they beat, ridiculed,
Scandalized, and manipulated me?*
But no one appears to hear,
To listen, to see, or to care
*Can't you see my kinky hair, my oval-shaped eyes,
My brown skin, and pretty smile
The uniqueness in my character,
Personality, and charisma?
They all make up my strengths, weaknesses,
Achievements, accomplishments,
Motivations, and dedications,*
But no one appears to hear,
To listen, to see, or to care

A young black girl with no voice,
No opinion, no ideas,
Nothing seems to matter
They say she's too fat, hair too nappy,
Words are unclear,
Skin has too much pigmentation
And she's a woman
They say she's too black to sit next to me,

Pain Is The Name of The Game

Too black to talk to me,
Too black to work in any establishment;
Most importantly,
She's too black to think for herself,
So let's think for her

We will tell her how to walk, what to wear,
How to speak, when to speak,
What to speak and where to speak
We will tell her how to do things our way,
She's too dumb to have a brain of her own

We will tell her how to move and when to move,
We will also cancel out people
That know more than us,
They may have a good influence on her
We can't allow that to happen,
We must keep her "brainwashed"
We will take from her, ruin her character,
And make her think she is worthless
We must capture her mind
If we say it to her over and over again,
It will become repetitive
And she will become programmed by us

A young black girl with no voice,
No opinion, no ideas,
Nothing seems to matter
But what they fail to realize is
This young black girl is
Too powerful to be bound by words
She's too powerful to be abused
Mentally, physically,
Spiritually, and emotionally

Nashya M. Williams

This young black girl is too educated to be naïve
This young black girl takes matters
Into her own hands
This young black girl has taken her life back
So she pushes herself to become
The young black girl
They never thought she would be
She decided to take the negatives
And turn them into positives,
Something they didn't know she was capable of

Fasting, praying, hoping, and believing
Are what priorities came to be
Suicidal thoughts, rages in anger,
Knowing that they would be better off
If she was dead than alive
The pain and suffering, the emotional damage,
The abandonment,
The hatred that she has overcome

She won't give you the satisfaction
Of visitation at her grave
Migraines and headaches, popping pain pills
To make it through the day
Head is in the clouds, mind is so free,
Body is in hell,
And the rest is history
It's not all a dream; it's reality
Many hate to talk about, tired of talking about,
Won't talk about it, but it's reality

So the next time you try to control
This young black girl
By stripping her of her dignity

Pain Is The Name of The Game

Just remember the unjust doesn't prosper
And karma is insane,
Misery loves everybody's company,
So where is your name?
Just hope it's not caught up in the rapture
When He says,
"Depart from me, I know you not,
You workers of iniquity"

Nashya M. Williams

The Silent Killer

Now this silent killer is not what you think
Crafting, masterminding, manipulating its victim,
Scrutinizing, circumcising, cannibalizing its victim
Walking back and forth, pacing the floor
Creating a strategic plan
Wondering how can they kill in silence
And mutilate the corpse
In the palm of their own two hands

Alone in a room with pure darkness
Being able to see the pure white walls,
Those walls aren't walls
Until they are painted in red,
And so forth, now let's move on

Now this silent killer is not what you think
Crafting, masterminding, manipulating its victim,
Scrutinizing, circumcising, cannibalizing its victim
No one knows the pain you feel
Until you have lashed out
Laughing at things that aren't even funny
Just to keep from crying out loud

What's wrong? Is everything OK?
You simply asked out of your mouth
If I told you how I truly feel,
Would you be able to handle it
Without airing it out?

Snapchat, Facebook, Instagram, I hide behind it all
I am the funny one you see who gets overlooked
As if I know it all

Pain Is The Name of The Game

But overall you sit in my face, laugh at me,
But yet you still don't see
That I'm human just like you are,
Chasing my dream at its highest peak

My emotions are like rollercoasters
That I need your ears to ride on,
But still you send me
To a psychiatric ward to depend on
Now this silent killer is not what you think
Crafting, masterminding, manipulating its victim,
Scrutinizing, circumcising, cannibalizing its victim
The victim that you see in front of you
Is looking right back at you,
But because you are blinded by my laughter,
You don't see me dying in my silence
Your attention is needed
And your words are comforting,
But because I'm entertaining,
You laugh harder than a hyena

Now this silent killer is not what you think
Crafting, masterminding, manipulating its victim,
Scrutinizing, circumcising, cannibalizing its victim
This victim died years ago;
However, you will never know
When it's all said and done
And the jokes have subsided,
You will then realize how dead I really am inside.

Nashya M. Williams

Misunderstood

I am misunderstood in so many ways,
You don't understand my uniqueness,
You don't understand my pain
God has created me in His own image
According to King James,
But the arguments of God being a certain image
Remains the same
Now I'm not here to argue
Whether God is black or white,
One thing is for certain,
I am misunderstood without a doubt

My opinions, my ideas,
The way I interpret different meanings
The way I style my hair to the clothes I wear,
You say it's condescending
You really don't understand me as a human being,
So why do you think I'm going to cooperate
With your silly strings?
Pulling me in different directions
Like a movie scene,
Casting, directing, and scripting
Every line that you see
But behind the scenes is just a puppet on the string,
Making me out to be what you want me to be

I am misunderstood in so many ways,
You don't understand my uniqueness,
You don't understand my pain
You don't understand my bluntness,
You think I'm too keen

Pain Is The Name of The Game

You don't understand my sarcasm,
You think I'm being mean
But when I'm off to the side
Observing my surroundings,
You think I'm too good to be surrounded
By different crowds and social groups
But you better take your eyes off of me
And keep them on Jesus
He's the one you need,
He's the one that can save you

Little old me, I'm just an observer
Feeling all the vibes
And watching all the spectators
Just because I'm quiet doesn't mean
I'm a pushover,
Let me say this again,
Just in case you've looked over
Little old me, I'm just an observer
Feeling all the vibes
And watching all the spectators
I am misunderstood in so many ways,
You don't understand my uniqueness,
You don't understand my pain

To love me is to know me,
To know me is to love me,
Yeah I know it's cliché, but it's a true statement
To love me is to know me,
To know me is to love me,
No this is not a silhouette, it's a true story
Now open your eyes and take a moment to realize,
We are all different people in our own eyes,

Nashya M. Williams

But the only eyes that matter are God's eyes
Minimize your faith then He will
Minimize your lifeline,

So keep your eyes on the prize and not mine
For I have come to realize,
Even though I'm misunderstood,
It is all right,
If you can see my heart,
Then you will see
Where understanding is found

Pain Is The Name of The Game

Nashya M. Williams

Pulsating Headaches

What triggers a headache?
The doctor says it's stress, lack of sleep,
Lack of nutrients, and lack of peace.
Lack of exercising, lack of understanding,
Lack of fluids, and anxiety
But what really triggers my headaches
Is something I can't explain.

The pulsating points of pressure
Constantly throbbing in my head
The constant motion of the whirlwind,
Traveling a thousand miles per hour,
Where does it end?

The opening and closing of my eyes,
Seeing sparkles and dark spots all at the same time,
When does it end?

MAKE IT STOP, MAKE IT STOP!

Day by day, minute by minute, hour by hour,
Second by second, the pulsating continues
Depression, anxiety, confusion
Is all a part of the menu
To be fed by someone who's not competent enough
To make sensible decisions,
Without having the temporary relief
Of pain medications

MAKE IT STOP, MAKE IT STOP!

What triggers a headache, you ask? Hmmm…

Pain Is The Name of The Game

Not knowing which way to go—left or right,
Even though left and right are different ways,
It all seems the same way with a pulsating headache

HOW CAN I MAKE IT STOP?

Antagonizing me with your different techniques,
Questioning me as if we are debating
As the trial jury
Short answers to let you know
I don't want to be bothered,
Head grows more and more by the hour

Not being mean in any way,
Hope you understand today is not my day
We all have days we don't want to be bothered,
Furthermore, this headache is
Continuously throbbing
Just because I'm not smiling
Doesn't mean I hate you,

I just have a pulsating headache
That's getting in the way
Of me making sensible decisions
Without the shortest response,
So I distance myself and lie down,
Hoping this headache will go away
Yet you follow me to see if I would sway
Your antagonizing techniques are making me angry,

Now I'm beginning to feel
The intentions of your techniques;
It's not even funny

Nashya M. Williams

When I go off, you wonder why did it come to this,
It's because my pulsating headaches
Had me seeing visions

MAKE IT STOP!

Pain Is The Name of The Game

Nashya M. Williams

Therapy

They say a mind is a terrible thing to waste
In reality many humans don't understand
How the human mind thinks
Women don't understand men,
Men don't understand women
Writing many books and plays on how to
Understand each other
Still no solution

I am no mind reader;
I don't know what you are thinking
Many people have stated this line
Without regurgitating
Assuming that you've solved the equation
To the human brain
No solution will end with you up in therapy
Speaking with a psychologist or a psychiatrist
Is all the same
One prescribes medication,
The other prescribes rehabilitation;
It's all the same
Although it's not a bad thing,
But what happens when you already know
The answers to your questions?

The medicine that was prescribed
Has now created delusions,
The rehabilitation that was prescribed
Now has you second-guessing
And realizing time was wasted
Clock's ticking, meter's rolling,

Pain Is The Name of The Game

And therapist continuously
Watches the time
To make sure that every second, minute,
And hour is counted,
And not to go over time

Therapy is what they told me I needed;
My problems were too big for them to deal with
Unlike any other human with the same issues,
They say therapy is the best decision for you

No one wants to listen to the same issues
Over and over again,
Let someone help you
Who's certified in that profession
I told you what I think and what you needed to do,
You don't want to listen to me,
A true friend that I am

If I didn't love you, I wouldn't tell you,
"Friend, get some help"
You are impatient and an emotional wreck
And I can't deal with that
You need to learn how to let go and let God;
It's out of your control
So let someone else help you;
Therapy should be your goal

But let me tell you about my issues
And let me borrow your tissues
My problems are enough for you to deal with
I know you are dealing with matters of the heart
Let's just skip right over that

Nashya M. Williams

And help me to get a new start,
I have the weight of the world on my shoulders,

So good friend
You give great sound advice, what's your opinion?
You know what, I'll just let go and let God
And let that be
But for you my friend, you need therapy
No I never said you were crazy
You just need therapy

Pain Is The Name of The Game

Nashya M. Williams

Dear Best Friend

Remember when we made a vow to never break,
No matter what life brought our way
We met through a mutual friend of ours,
Who we are no longer friends with,
But hey we were just teenagers back then
We lived around the corner from each other,
Literally it was one street over from one another
I remember the first time meeting your mother,
Greeted her properly and asked for you
The look she gave me was like, *who are you*?
Not knowing she was pregnant at that time,
I told you and you said, "Oh girl, that's fine."
I remember coming home
From middle and high school
Exiting the same bus,
Standing there discussing what annoyed us the most
Then we would go to our houses
And call each other on the telephone,
Talked for hours until we got in trouble

Time went on and we became closer friends,
Not knowing where we would end
We made plans to name our kids after each other,
Then at the time we made a vow to one another
Remember when we made a vow to never break,
No matter what life brought our way?
Time went on and we grew up,
Graduating from the same high school
Was a success
Then we went our separate ways
To pursue our careers,

Pain Is The Name of The Game

But that's when I noticed our friendship
Was coming to an end
We tried our best to keep in touch,
But controlling relationships became a bit much

I was losing more and more of you,
But you would just brush it off
Where were you when I needed you the most?
You would say selfishness is what I made my home
You were like the sister I never had growing up,
So I cherished you and held you close to me
Because you understood my struggles

Thirteen years of friendship
Have gone down the drain
What happened to us?
Why the all of a sudden change?
When we made a vow to never break,
No matter what life brought our way
Our friendship will never be the same,
No you were not my lover,
You were truly my best friend
I called you more than I called my own mother,
Because I needed your truest opinion

Jealousy, deceit, lies was the game that was played,
I saw it on many days
Three years have passed and your face
I still don't see
I thought we were better than that;
I guess that was a lie that is plain to see
Can we say it's pride on both parts,
Or can we say our time is just up?

Nashya M. Williams

Remember when we made a vow to never break,
No matter what life brought our way
Thirteen years of friendship
Have gone down the drain
What happened to us?
Why the all of a sudden change?
Questions in my head still remain, like *why* and *how*
Or is it a mystery that will never get solved?
I have no regrets on what has evolved

I will always love you,
In my heart you will always stay
That's something that will never change

I have accepted that our friendship
Has ran its course,
As we can see our feelings,
There is no remorse
I wish you nothing but the best,
Peace love and happiness
But most importantly
Congratulations on your greatest success

Pain Is The Name of The Game

Nashya M. Williams

Backstabber

The knife in my back is so deep,
The more you talk the more I bleed
The more you talk the more it is deep,
Deep seated in my spine,
Pivoting every angle, hitting every defined line
I ask you why my friend, my brother,
The one I knew like no other
I had your back, your front, your side,
But it's clear to see
You've put a knife in mine

When you were down and out,
I fed you, I clothed you,
And I gave you advice over and over
Now you're talking, smiling,
And praising my name all while
You have a knife in my back,
Things are just not the same

Friend look at me, I'm dying
Look at all the blood stains
As if we are on the battlefield's frontline
NO NO NO NO NO, you're no friend of mine
I've used you for my own gain
To get to my own divine
You thought I was your friend,
You've trusted me with your life,
But I'm really your enemy dressed in disguised

Have you ever heard of wolves in sheep's clothing?
That was me all along, your friend and your brother,

Pain Is The Name of The Game

You are oh so very wrong
Your life is so much better than mine;
You've tried and succeeded with all of your might
I've mimicked your life and look at mine;
I've repeatedly failed time after time
Your nice car, your pretty house,
That picket fence looks oh so nice

Your great career, your big family
Who do you think you are to get ahead of me?
Jealousy is my real name,
Envy is the name of the game
I've played your life like chess in a board game

Now you look at me in shock and enraged,
But remember this knife is in your back
And it's due to my own personal gain
This knife represents all of the pain you've caused
Every success, every fall through,
You've won them all
As I deeply insert this knife
Deep seated in your spine,
Pivoting every angle hitting every defined line
It gives me great joy and pleasure
To see you die a slow death
Victory is mine just like the gospel song says
So the next time you should be wise
And choose your friends carefully,
Or you will end up with a wolverine as an enemy
Backstabber is what they call me

Nashya M. Williams

Lack of Support

Your mind is bottled with so many ideas
Your emotions are roaring, yet your body is still
Your eyes are closed, you see your success,
Whether you're a news anchor reporter
Or a seamstress sewing your first dress
Success comes in many ways and different forms,
But the lack of support is what will have you torn

You've shared your ideas,
You've shown part of your work,
But the response you receive
Carries the deepest hurt

"Congratulations", "I'll support you",
"I have your back"
"Let me know if you need me",
"Keep up the good work"
"For you, I will check into that"
Those words are very kind,
Very generous, very considerate,
Yet very cliché, very suitable,
And very contradicting
Success comes in many ways and different forms,
But the lack of support is what will have you torn

Now we all know the adult industry
Is a multi-billion-dollar industry,
You will throw your money for a smile
And a thank you
You will spend fifty dollars on drinks,
One hundred dollars for a lap dance,
But won't even support your own family

Pain Is The Name of The Game

The struggle is real, the hustle game is strong,
Not knowing anyone's strategies
Truth hurts, but the words are like thorns
Pillow wet with tears, nobody hears you
Because your thoughts are just thoughts
But what happens when those thoughts become
A million-dollar franchise off of lack of support?

Now you're my best friend, my coolest brother
Wanting to know how can you
Become my business partner

For success comes in many ways
And different forms,
But the lack of support is what will have you torn
Your voice is wanted, ideas are appreciated,
Your genuine feelings will not get depleted
For your first panel of judges on your way to the top
Are the ones who will critique you
Whether you want it or not
Support you or not, they have an influence anyway,
Because they are your family

Nashya M. Williams

Black and White

Two neutral colors that can't be erased,
Two neutral colors that can't be mixed
To create its base
There are black and white countertops,
Black and white sheets,
Black and white news
Black and white people, no that's not the case
Society states black and white
To distinguish our race

We are people of color, but not in their eyes,
We are people whose character has been demised
They are killing our children
Because of the color of their skin,
They are killing our women
Because of their African descent
They are killing our men, due to what's within,
Whether it's their talents, masculinity,
Sexual orientation, or just because
They are black men

Two neutral colors that can't be erased,
Two neutral colors that can't be mixed
To create its base
White people are not white,
It's just the pigmentation of their skin
They are not the reason people of color
Have hatred within
Now I understand slavery way back then,
How our ancestors were beaten
Bruised with marks to match their melanin

Pain Is The Name of The Game

Caucasian people go through similar struggles
As our people of color,
Addicted to heroin and cocaine
Sounds so very familiar
We grew up with broken homes,
We become adults and raise our children
In broken homes
The cycle repeats itself, creating self hate,
Then we blame it on other people
And cultures of a different race

The famous saying is
"The white man is trying to hold us down",
Truth of the matter is we as people
Are holding our own selves down
We are like crabs in a bucket
With this black-on-black crime,
What happened to "Black Lives Matter"
Or was that just a black and white sign

Two neutral colors that can't be erased,
Two neutral colors that can't be mixed
To create its base
"Little black boys and black girls
Will be able to join hands
With little white boys and white girls
As sisters and brothers"
Are the words of Dr. Martin Luther King
For divided we part, united we stand,
Fight for your beliefs,
Or you will fall for anything

"We the People" is written boldly
In the Preamble of the U.S. Constitution

Nashya M. Williams

"We hold these truths to be self-evident,
That all men are created equal;
That they are endowed by their creator
With certain inalienable rights
That among these are life, liberty,
And the pursuit of happiness"
Is written in the American
Declaration of Independence

Black and white has yet to be distinguished,
Except for the ink that was used
For the words to be written
So this crime with killing our people has to stop
Police brutality, ongoing riots,
Parents killing children,
Children killing parents
Self-inflictions have to stop
For we are one nation, under God, indivisible,
With liberty, and justice for all

Pain Is The Name of The Game

Nashya M. Williams

Missing You

He was a young black male at the age of 26
He wanted to fit in although he was different
Doctors put a life expectancy date
When he was born
Mentally that didn't stop him from growing

He grew up knowing that he was different
Health issues are what made his life relentless
Homeschooled as a student because he was sickly
This young black male was very independent
Smelled good, looked good, and cooked very well
Managed to live on his own without any help

Even though he was labeled disabled in the system
He was not a man who was incompetent
He was a young black male at the age of 26
He wanted to fit in although he was different

I met him at the age of 18, he was either 14 or 15
We laughed and talked through sunrises,
Revealing secrets I would never mention
As we grew up in age his health started to fade
He went to the hospital numerous times,
But always bounced back like the champ he was
Keeping me updated with every date,
What the doctors said,
And how he hated it

He was a young black male at the age of 26
He wanted to fit in although he was different
On this very day, I received a call
He told me he was at the hospital,

Pain Is The Name of The Game

But he hoped it wouldn't be long
He was wrong—with his visits
They became very frequent
Even though he was at the hospital
He was getting weaker
He updated me with current events,
And what led him to his visits
He delivered some news which left me torn
I encouraged him to stay strong and remember
What the doctor said when he was born
Remembering the greatest times
And accomplishments of his life
And to always keep up the good fight

The cancer wasn't getting any better
As time went on
He stopped answering my phone calls,
I became annoyed

He was a young black male at the age of 26
He wanted to fit in although he was different
Finally, he gave me a call, I told him how I felt,
Not knowing what went on
He said he had to distance himself from people
Because he was deteriorating within his own skin
He said, "I have to be honest,
I'm not getting any better,
I have to tell you this news
Because you are my sister"
He told me not only did he have cancer
That was failing him,
But he was diagnosed with HIV
And it messed with him mentally

Nashya M. Williams

Devastated I was and began to cry silently,
Lifting his spirits to the best of my ability
Sad news is we were distant,
But the phone calls were very consistent

He was a young black male at the age of 26
He wanted to fit in although he was different
He informed me of his aches and pains
As they grew stronger
I never gave up on encouraging him,
Even though I would hang up and cry hysterically
He told me how he felt about death
And how he wasn't scared
How he was ready, he was tired of trying,
And tired of fighting

Two months after his birthday he gave up the fight,
Cancer and HIV took his might
He battled with different ailments his whole life
He was ready and tired, he explained to me
As an early sign
I didn't think it would come so soon
For us to say goodbye

He wasn't just a good friend, he was my brother
The one I met at 18 along with the others
Even though our moment together was very short
I will always cherish our bond we created the most

He was a young black male at the age of 26
A young black male that will always be missed

Pain Is The Name of The Game

Nashya M. Williams

Pain Is The Name of The Game

Piercing eyes, broken hearts, convicted minds
Sweating palms, emotions rise, self-inflictions,
No compromising
Pain is created by the words that are spoken,
Pain is created by the actions provoked
It's all fun and games until someone gets hurt,
Then it's time to get back, time for war
Strategies and plans are submitted
On how retaliation is acquitted
The game of cat and mouse takes place,
You run and hide, but forget your family
Family gets blazed, but no one gets hurt,
Pop, pop, pop over thirty times,
Ha ha that was berserk
No lives lost, you should be grateful
Once you're found, that bullet will come after you,
It's all in the making
Word on the street is you live by the sword,
You die by the sword, that's the motto
Wounds are created, scars are the cause of it,
Torture is repeated, and wounds are reopened
The pain is rooted at the seed,
Hatred then rises, envy blossoms,
And produces the scent of greed
Red and blue veins are punctured,
The liquid runs from every angle,
Nothing to stop the flow
Seeing dark spots suddenly, eyes are closed,
Heart stops
Sending signals to other organs to stop,
No more liquid, no more pain

GAME OVER!

Pain Is The Name of The Game

Nashya M. Williams

Love

Is

Unfair

"Relationships"

Pain Is The Name of The Game

Nashya M. Williams

__Lust Is Love, Love Is Lust__

Do we really know the difference between the two?
Many people get in relationships based on lust,
Many people lust for a relationship and say it is love
You take them out based on their intellect,
Your emotions increase
Based on their physical connect,
After one night the words *I love you* come about
Someone is taking it literal
While the other one is lusting
For more of their insides

What was perceived as love was really lust,
No more dates, no more outings,
Just erotic interaction in strange places,
Now you want to become exclusive with that person
To save faces,
Someone is falling deeper in love,
While the other one is deeply in lust
The argument begins,
Because the other person is missing out

They are starting to fill a void
That was filled with love,
So they thought
The deeper the interaction
Of body chemistry takes place,
The more of a disconnect they become
Emotions rise and tears fall, for more of their love
And the other is aggravated
For the lack thereof their lust

Pain Is The Name of The Game

Fifteen years later,
Still playing the game of cat and mouse,
The cat wants love and the mouse wants lust

The conversation of marriage comes up
To put a seal on their love,
The other denies because
They no longer desire their lust
The lust has been found and given to another one,
The other is left broken

What was perceived to be love was lust
Because lust was married already to their true love,
For thirty years
The love that was once there
Is no longer there Between the two
Although both are joined in matrimony,
Both are wanting out
But because so many years were invested,
No one wants to test it;
Love is lost, lust is present
Love is lust; lust is love was the reason

Nashya M. Williams

In Between the Sheets

Sometimes things are not meant to be,
You offered to cook, clean, and to be his peace
The only thing he wants
Is you in between the sheets
He keeps expressing over and over
How you please him
How he gets happy in ways that he can't explain,
Your kisses and touch still remains,
All while you want his last name

He keeps saying he doesn't want a relationship,
But you catch him online
Changing his profile on the dating websites
Time after time
Looking for a wife/soul mate he states,
But to you he's not on there much
Just something to do when he's bored at work

He's divorced from his ten-year marriage
From his first wife;
Because you know his heart,
You try to become his second wife
You offered to cook, clean, and to be his peace;
The only thing he wants
Is you in between the sheets

So to make him see your point,
You stop giving him what he wants,
Oh the pleasure that he craved is cut off,
Because you are feeling misused at this point
You continuously confront him

Pain Is The Name of The Game

And ask him questions about his intentions,
He constantly says he wants friends with benefits,
But you show him there is more to you
Than what's on the surface

You can be his wife you know,
Like he stated on his profile
He flip flops so quickly like it's a style

One minute he's open to the idea of a wife,
The next he just wants to chase that high
Of being with a woman for her innocence
And when he's ready,
He will give her permission to access his heart

Saying one thing and doing another,
So you stop feeding his pleasure,
Now he's fallen back to seek others
Leaving you to pick up the pieces,
Because you've fallen for him for different reasons
He says you stopped giving him pleasure,
So he lost interest
That's what happened in his previous adventure,
The fact you stopped reminded him of his past
And because of that you can't last

He tells you to get back out there and try it again,
He's just chillin', he doesn't make a good husband
You know his interest has gone,
But you stay in touch
Hoping his mindset will change
And you two can correlate together that much

Nashya M. Williams

Instead he gets what he wanted,
Which is a relationship from another
Left you feeling that you were just a number
All because you took a stand,
You knew you deserved more
Worth more than just a score

He stopped all contact with you
And you have come to terms
With how it ends,
Those feelings are pushed aside
With a patch on them
Then one day you see a comment online
With him mentioning his female lover worldwide
You think to yourself, *why not me?*
I offered to cook, clean, and to be your peace,
But all you wanted was me in between the sheets

Karma has a way of finding its place,
It comes when you least expect it
And hits you in the face,
He will feel the pain that you feel deep within,
Playing mind games just to win
One day you will cross paths again,
Then he will notice you,
But by that time it will be too late
The one he took for granted will be shining
Like a diamond by her new mate
Sometimes things are just not meant to be,
One man's trash is another man's treasure;
He will be your peace and make you his queen

Pain Is The Name of The Game

Nashya M. Williams

Intimidation

You said you loved me and adored me
Why must you intimidate me to restore me
You've abandoned me and left me broken
Shattered me like a stainless glass in the hallway

You left me and came back only to say *I'm sorry*
Your tone of voice started out smooth,
We made amends but you left again
Years have passed then you return,
Only to say *I'm sorry*
The words are now a little more stern
Raising your voice for me to see your point
Tension rises, I get quiet,
And let you finish your exhort

If looks could kill,
I would be dead by the piercings in your eyes
You look into my spirit with a profound lens
To captivate my soul
The love I once had for you is no more

I'm a delicate flower, you overlooked my petals
Your intimidation caused me to wither
Pouring out your charming words doesn't save me
From the catastrophe of your actions
I've cried for your attention and affection,
But there was no reception

The amount of respect you give me is none at all,
You expect me to change my feelings all in one call

Pain Is The Name of The Game

Now you are a changed man
With a consecutive story
Sorry isn't enough, you've been gone for years
And returned with the same old tears

Intimidation is being superior
Like preying on the weak
I will no longer be detained by your soul
You've chained to me
I release myself from your imprisoned mind
No longer can you return with the same old prowl,
No more apologies, no more cries

Intimidation is no longer a threat to my sanity

Nashya M. Williams

Loyalty

Where does your loyalty lie?
One minute I love you, the next minute I miss you,
And the final conclusion is I'm in a relationship
This circle of inconsistency has become a trend
For the style of our friendship,
Saying things that are matters of the heart,
Encouraging words, and heartfelt thoughts

Heartfelt analogies to describe
How great of a friendship we have,
Telling me I will always be the one you adore,
Because our friendship to you
Means that much more
Questioning our friendship
As to why it has yet to be elevated,
We have such a great understanding of each other
Why can't we be together?

Only to find out weeks later on my timeline
Your post is the first I see,
Smiling and posing with someone who isn't me
In a relationship it states, confusion hits me;
It was just the other day I heard you say,
"You are special to me and that will never change"

I go off on an emotional rampage
"Calm down," you say
"It happened so suddenly, nothing was planned"
I forgave you and let you be
Only for you to return so suddenly,
So now we are back at square one
With your heartwarming thoughts

Pain Is The Name of The Game

The cycle repeats itself time and time again,
Exchange words that we never should've said,
Apologies are set forth on more than one occasion

We finally agreed to be honest from the start,
No more hidden secrets,
After all, we are just friends, right?

We decided to explore our thoughts of each other,
Random dates, I thought was very clever,
Expecting so much more from a long-term friend
Since grade school,
Suddenly became a stranger, someone I never knew

Realizing dates were not of our nature,
So friends we decided to stay to make it easier
Having the mutual understanding
Of no more secrets,
We laugh and talk about the rollercoaster ride
Of your relationship

Time goes on, friendship still stands strong
When asked about the update of your relationship,
It was no more
Here we go again; it never fails
Those heartwarming thoughts
Of yours continuously prevails

"Why can't we be together?" you asked again.
"It's because I don't trust you," I added in

Your actions to me said let me show you different,
Never crossed the line of physical pleasure,

Nashya M. Williams

Mentally I was locked into you,
You were the one I sought after
Being down and out I cheered you up,
We ate pizza and drunk wine
To take your mind off of life,
Now your strength is back,
Friends yet we still remain,
Encouraging each other to be the best at life
Beating all the odds

You gave me a kiss on the forehead
As you spoke the words *I love you*,
Agreeing to help each other out spiritually
To the best of our ability
The New Year came in,
Found out you were engaged

Never knew you two got back together,
The secrets we promised
Not to hold from each other
No I didn't hear it from the grapevine,
Sad to say I found out on my timeline,
It was posted within another post as a comment,
My intentions were to comment
On that post of positive words,
Had no idea I would see that picture
Of your proposal

There were no signs of seeing
That you were in love with someone else,
Although I'm not surprised,
Your lies were a part of your lifestyle
I asked you was it true, you confirmed with a reply,
So my question to you is,
"Where does your loyalty lie?"

Pain Is The Name of The Game

Obviously not with me,
You would've respected my wishes
And told me that you were very happy

Happy with someone else
Who you felt deserved to be your wife,
Someone you don't have to struggle with
Inside and out
I would've respected and accepted it much better,
Being that you never were going to tell me,
Questioned my every opinion
Of your morals and character,
There is nothing else to be said, but I wish you well
In due time, she will see your mask revealed.

Nashya M. Williams

The Game Has Changed

This new millennium has changed the game,
What happened to men who used to court women,
And called them by their names?
Opening the door and holding their hand
As a sign of interests,
Walking them to the door and a kiss on the forehead
As a sign of *I will miss you*

Late night conversations on the phone,
Ending with the words I love you,
A three-word phrase that was used on both parties
With deep emotions
Meeting the parents was taking it a step further,
Getting the father's approval
For her hand in marriage
Without a question

Continued date nights with a bouquet of flowers,
Leaving no doubts in the minds of each other of any
Existence of another
This new millennium has changed the game,
Now we all act the same
Do unto others as you would have them
To do unto you
Is not an option,
We are playing get back with fire,
And losing lives in the process

Time is no longer of the essence;
It's our way or the highway, so make your decision
Men no longer know your name,

Pain Is The Name of The Game

But by the association of your character,
No one wants love, just fifteen minutes of pleasure,
Fifteen minutes of fame
Equals to fifteen millions of cheddar

They go after what they see on TV,
The get-rich schemes and a hot reputation
Is how they get them,
Throwing up peace signs and gang signs
Because you have it all together,
Selling your soul for a bowl of Lucky Charms
Which ends your career

Too much energy is being placed
Into the wrong activities,
Posting on social media just
To show your insecurities,
Men meeting women and women
Meeting men for quickies,
Because their main squeeze at home
Isn't making ends meet

No more trying to get to know each other
On a personal level,
We must be friends with benefits first
Before we can talk about being together
Then you wonder how
And why you caught that disease,
Because the person you linked up with
Was on a mission,
A mission to make sure you would never become
Submissive to that person

Nashya M. Williams

Women are turning to women because they are tired
Of being taken for granted,
Men are turning to men for deeper satisfaction
Why does it have to be friends with benefits
Before we can deeply connect
With one another mentally,
Taking the time to know each other sacredly,
Before we connect with one another intimately
Remember when men used to court women
For their attention?
Now women are busting it wide open
To gain their attention,
Leaving the men no reason to court women
The game has changed its positions

Pain Is The Name of The Game

Nashya M. Williams

I Apologize

A woman has a deck of cards that's been dealt,
She has to figure it out the best way she knows how
Some of those cards don't make sense,
So now she has to go off of her own instinct,
Growing up in a home without a father,
Being sexually abused by her stepfather

Mother is on drugs,
So she has to grow up very quickly,
Checking into her motherly instincts
To raise her siblings,
Selling her body to make ends meet,
Fingerprinted in the system to get assistance
Three meals a day, a cart, and a blanket,
Worrying that she won't get out to see her siblings,
Siblings are going from care to care in the system,
She returns back to them
Just to find out she's evicted,
Sad part is she's only eleven
So she grows up looking for someone
Who can help her,
But the only thing she knows
Is what she's been living,

Yes genuine men have treated her nice
A time or two,
But how can she trust you when pain
Is the only thing she knew
Now every brother that attempts to love her
Is shattered,

Pain Is The Name of The Game

Because they don't understand
How she can be so bitter,
Now she has a label:
The typical "angry black woman,"
Judging her without learning her struggles

All they see is a beautiful exterior
Of their physical attraction
For that woman,
Not realizing the interior is corrupted
With massive hate and rejection,

Any point can be a trigger point in her case,
She has grown into a beautiful butterfly,
But those issues never escaped

Now she longs for someone
Who can hold her and keep her safe,
Not use and abuse her at his own stake,
She doesn't allow too many people
To get close to her space,
So you come up with different names
To bring her shame

What you see is a woman who is shut down,
You try to be that man to her
But she doesn't know how,
To let you be that man to comfort her from all harm,
Know that in your arms is what she needs,
In your chest is where she can breathe

So instead of sticking it out,
You run to another race to engage

Nashya M. Williams

The uniqueness and nurturing they may bring
What a fairytale they betrayed
Took you for everything you made,
From the houses to the cars
To the pensions in the bank,
Now you're ready to come back to your race,
Because you've made a mistake,
Wanting her to help you pick up the pieces
That the other race created

In your eyes, she was an angry black woman,
But it was her own race that helped her discover,
The drugs, the rape, the prostitution, and the rage
It was you, black man, that she only knew
She trusted you with her heart, but you blew it

Now her heart is so guarded within a cage,
No one has the key so there it remains
But all you see is an angry black woman
Because you didn't personally vandalize her space,
But it was your kind that made her that way,
So now she thinks that all men are dogs,
Because no one was able to stand to her and not fall

But all you see is an angry black woman,
Get to know her background,
Before placing a label on this woman
For that alone, I want to apologize to the black men,

I apologize for your vindictive black woman
You ended up with
She is only showing you
What she was taught within,

Pain Is The Name of The Game

Her ruler was vindictive to whomever
He/she was with,
That black woman saw what
Was gained from that character,
And now you have to suffer because you love her

For that alone, I want to apologize to the black men,
I apologize for your lazy black woman
You ended up with
She started out being that wonder woman
You saw within your origin,
Now she's jobless, no meals, no clean clothes,
And no clean house
She always comes to you with her hand out

Black man, she's only doing what she's been told,
Her influencer has warned her about you
She saw that you are a good man
And was taught to take advantage of you
She was taught how to get you,
But once she's got you,
She was also taught on how to trick you
Now you're stuck with her because you love her,
Ruining your character
Because she was influenced by another

For that alone, I want to apologize to the black men,
I apologize for your abusive black woman
You ended up with
You see she encountered abuse
By her mother and father,
So her revenge is to take it out on
The innocent black man she encounters

Nashya M. Williams

She hits you, she breaks you down,
She acts as if you don't exist,
She tells the world your business,
Because that's just who she is,
So you take the good and the bad of this woman,
But you're stuck with her because you love her

I apologize, black men,
That black women are deceiving,
Manipulating, and condescending
I apologize for the broken promises and the lies,
The built up anger inside
I apologize, black men,
That black women force your hand to
Turn to another race,
To make you feel your own race
Being created was a mistake

See we as human beings can only
Teach other human beings
What we were taught,
So as an adult you can either
Live with those flaws or not,
But don't put a label on a woman
Without knowing her thoughts,
She's not just one angry black woman
That you've come across,
All women aren't angry, they just need guidance,
So guide her, black man,
If she's willing to be guided,

If not, leave her alone completely
And move to another to embrace

Pain Is The Name of The Game

All black women are not out to hurt you,
There are some that have been trained
To nurture you
And comfort you

Black men you are Nubian kings
And should be well respected,
Study that black woman a little more,
Before making a quick decision

In order to understand someone,
You must know and understand their background,
Stop labeling black women to hype the crowd
An angry black woman is a typical rant,
But if you learn to embrace that woman,
She'll be that one that you will never forget,
She will show you all the love and care
That a woman can give,
Just give her a chance and don't treat her no less,
For that angry black woman can turn into
That angel from heaven you won't regret

Nashya M. Williams

Love Yourself

Learn to love yourself,
Before you learn to love someone else
How many times must those words be played,
In order for real love to take place?
Countless nights you spend crying,
Wondering when your love will appear,
Everyone is posting on Facebook and Instagram
Like their partner is real

I'm not amused by your quick marriage
Or your twenty-five years of unmarried relationship
Because the Bible says
"Be ye not unequally yoked together
With unbelievers
For what fellowship hath righteous
With unrighteousness?
And what communion hath light with darkness?"
Stated in 2 Corinthians 6:14

Every joint hand in matrimony doesn't mean
They are meant to be married,
Ray Charles was a blind man,
But even he could see deception
Even God himself told you not to do it,
And then you wonder why,
You wake up every day
With physical bruises to the eye

"Learn to love yourself,
Before you learn to love someone else,"
Says the married woman of thirty-five years,
Been cheated on for twenty-five years,

Pain Is The Name of The Game

Smiling and cheesing for the whole world to see,
Going home to her husband lying in beds separately

"Learn to love yourself,
Before you learn to love someone else,"
Says the divorced woman of two years

Found out your husband
wasn't all he was cracked up to be,
You separated yourself from the whole world
Because you were so "happily married"
Now you're looking like Mary J Blige's
'Not Gon' Cry' video,
Black scarf, black shades, and black lipstick
Praying, pleading, and asking God
Why did he leave so quick

"You don't need a man," says an unmarried woman
In a relationship of fifteen years,
Putting up with his shenanigans on a daily basis,
Just to say you have a man
He proposed to you within those five years,
But he has no intentions on marrying you,
Which is a part of his plan,
So you post for the world to see you
And your boo so happy,
While fighting off every female
That knows your boo,
Just as well as you do

"You don't need a man,"
Says an unhappily married woman of ten years,
He's always gone and you're always home,

Nashya M. Williams

Now you're seeking companionship
Of another married man,
Who won't leave his home
Learn to love yourself,
Before you learn to love someone else
Is so cliché,
I wish women would stop telling other women that
To make them behave

You don't need a man
Is another statement of cover up
Woman that was your choice
To link up with that man;
Not mine,
So don't try to patronize my mind
To cover up what's inside

All men aren't dogs,
Just like all women aren't female dogs,
We are two human beings of the opposite sex
Just trying to get along
If it doesn't work out between you two,
Just move on and find you a new boo,
No need to hold malice in your heart
And giving out bitter advice to single
Women who want a fair shot

If it's too much for you to handle,
You can always leave
The same way you signed yourself in,
You can sign yourself out,
That's called "The Marriage Time Clock"
Johnnie Taylor said, "It's cheaper to keep her,"
I beg to differ

Pain Is The Name of The Game

The longer you stay, the bitter your heart,
The longer you stay that bitterness comes out,
The longer you stay, the unhappier you will be,
Then "I don't need a man" will become
Part of your vocabulary

Men are needed in multiple areas of women's lives,
If it wasn't so, they wouldn't exist,
Even the word women can't be completely spelled
Without adding men on the end
Learn to love yourself,
Before you learn to love someone else
What does that mean,
Because I've loved myself enough
To know what I need

I knew I needed determination
To find the purpose in my life
I knew I needed to focus
On that certain goal in my life
I knew I needed education to advance in my career
I knew I needed to gain more energy
To raise my seed,
With or without the father, I am needed
I have to be there to nurture without a reason

I knew I needed guidance,
So I chose to be in a positive environment to do so
I knew I needed the strength,
So I gained a prayer life for that to be so
If I didn't love myself,
I would've killed myself a long time ago,
Even when he said "No,"

Nashya M. Williams

I would have proceeded to go forth
In the act anyway
How dare you preach to me
What you don't practice,
You hypocrite,
Trying to stop me from gaining happiness
With your magic tricks
Your magic tricks of words
To cause witchcraft in my mind
To think negatively in my mind,
And transfer those feelings
Deep down on the inside
I do love myself more than you know,
Based on your situation,
The word love you will never know

Single women continue to build yourself
And rise to the top,
For your worth is more than just
Another bitter woman's advice
Know that you are valued more than what you see,
That king will come and value you
Beyond your beliefs,
It is not impossible for you to have a man,
But it is important for you to know God's plan

Dare to be different, that way your relationship
Will be undistinguished
Show the bitter women that every woman and man
Is not the same
I love you, single women,
Just keep doing your thing
One of these days you will get your ring,
And you make sure that your ring means everything!

Pain Is The Name of The Game

Nashya M. Williams

A Hard Pill to Swallow

I don't know how to express this any other way
But on paper,
Because if I tell you how I truly feel,
Then there goes the judging
We've grown so much in so many ways,
Until time apart seems to be the best way for us
To communicate

I was told I'm no longer a part of your circle,
So I have to accept
She helped me to understand
The old person I'm looking for
No longer exists
The new person is full of bliss, new adventures,
Full of romance, and happiness

The new person has found her place in life
And because of it,
She has no time for outsiders
It's a hard pill to swallow,
Not because you're happy,
But because I'm not in that circle of life
I was the first person you told,
The person you would ask an opinion from,
The person you would see for a laugh or two

Now I'm the person you decide
If you should tell or not,
The person you choose to avoid and keep distant
Carefully not causing a scene
And to not point out the obvious

Pain Is The Name of The Game

She told me she doesn't want me to revert back
To where I healed from,
To allow one somebody to make me feel bounded,
She said she doesn't know what kind of
Hold you have on me,
But I need to let that thing go
And let the rest be history

You were more than just a best friend,
You were my sister to the end,
Many won't understand our friendship,
So they can only say what they feel
Thirteen years is a long time to be best friends,
Even longer to be reunited
And still feel like distant cousins

You have no idea the many nights I've cried,
Wondering why I felt so alone at that time
What did I do that was so bad to make you leave
And not say goodbye
We've had light discussions about this topic,
But I still feel there is something deeper
That you aren't discussing

The pain still remains
Because you were a part of my life,
But as soon as my life changed you did the same
I thought our bond was thicker than water,
Seeing our high school friendships
Mature like mortar,
They're closer than they've ever been
Regardless of their statuses,

Nashya M. Williams

Not understanding why distance
Is the thing that matters

She said I was so happy,
All I kept saying was I got my friend back,
Then weeks later my voice changed
To be reminded of what took place
She said you have to understand where she is in life,
The person you want back has bailed out
I know it's a hard pill to swallow, but she's right,
The only thing I can do now
Is love you from a distance
Like she advised

Yes it's a hard pill to swallow,
Because I have so much to talk about,
Attempting to be best friends with the men I date,
Who don't care to listen
They don't care about me growing my hair,
Trying to find the next deals and bargains
Which shirt goes with which skirt,
Or to find the best shoes to match the outfit

Now I understand when men say she's changed,
She's not the same person I married,
She's now a pain
My response was you knew what you were getting
When you married her,
Now all of sudden you want an exchange
We all change, whether it's for the better or worse
As a whole,
Life challenges grow
True friends remain the same,
For they were there before your name changed

Pain Is The Name of The Game

You thought I never cared,
I was trying to deal with
The instability of my emotions,
The coming and the going,
Because of the bond we shared,
Knowing the many friendships I've had faded,
Due to their status changing

I'm not married, I get it,
But why do I become a stranger
And when hard times arise,
They seem to find my number,
I've lost a lot of friends
Because of that and because of that
I will never look back

My sister that I grew up with is a different story;
We made memories galore
You always seek that person
To know you inside and out,
The one who tells you you're wrong without a smile

The one you tell your darkest secrets to
And you know they won't get out
I'm still healing, although it's a process
I will pray and pray until God
Completely heals my heart
It's just a hard pill to swallow about how life turns out

Nashya M. Williams

A Change of Heart

The love was there for many years
Throughout the years, the love has been tested
Infidelity took the place in where love once was
The many candidates that took place
In the triangle of lust
Is no longer a must

The residue of hurt from the many incidents
Lingers to the growing years
Lies, deceit, trust, anger, and questions
Are in the heart of the parties
As they move forward to make it work
Conversations and actions
Trigger the motives of the previous incidents,
How can moving forward be the initiative
When the triggers are reversible

Scents and emotions are unforgettable,
The events that have transpired seem unforgiving
To say I love you all in the same breath
But show how much the love is there
By entertaining someone else

When will enough be enough for the parties to see
They need each other more than anything
Due to the long hardship years the growing pains,
The growing tears,
Makes it difficult to satisfy one another passionately

The fights, the arguments, the kick-outs,
The saying things they really don't mean
Because they are worn out

Pain Is The Name of The Game

What happened to the joy and happiness
That brought them together,
The main attraction of what made them stay connected

Infidelity played a big part
Now they have a change of heart,
Not allowing anyone to break them apart
Although it's been many years of the unity,
A change of heart is what brings them purity

Realizing they need each other internally,
No one can understand them better than how they
Have grown to know
Hard work and dedication has brought them this far,
But a change of heart will heal the scars

The love is now back in the picture,
Although it never left, it was the change of heart,
That reunited them to make amends

Nashya M. Williams

The

Process

of

Healing

"Healing the Pain"

Pain Is The Name of The Game

Nashya M. Williams

To Be Free

You want to know what it's like to be free
It comes from deep down on the inside, no one can see
It's like the blood that runs through your veins
That can only be plucked and felt
To get ready for drawing
By a needle that fits

You want to know what it's like to be free
Soaring high like an eagle in the sky
With nothing on the brain,
On cloud nine as they would say
The numbness feeling in your body
As if there is nothing flowing
The emptiness in your mind as if there is nothing there
Breathing fresh air although you are not outside
To be free is the intensifying but yet settling feeling

Free from the hurt and pain
Free from the mental restraints
Free from the words that scar
Free from the broken hearts
Free from the shattered relationships
Free from the dysfunctional families
Free from the lack thereof
Free from the life of struggles
Free from the demons we created
Free from the world of hatred

Being free from the bondage and chains
Forgiving others and the victory you will gain
The freedom to forgive and not judge inwardly
To focus on your dreams and not be irritated
By the irrelevant events

Pain Is The Name of The Game

>To accomplish the goals
>And to be excited about the hard work
>You've set forth to birth it
>
>You want to know what it is like to be free
>Let it all go and you will see
>Freedom is where you need to be

Nashya M. Williams

A Mother's Love

A mother's love for her child will never die,
No matter how hard she tries
There is a connection that is indescribable for words
A connection that no man with the naked eye can see,
Because that child came from her loins,
He or she was created to be
A mother's love for her child will never die,
No matter how hard she tries
Society says your child is a thief, murderer,
Crack head, drug addict,
Thug, prostitute, stripper, instigator,
Liar, cheater, manipulator,
A woman and a man beater
Society asks how can you love a child
With that many flaws,
The hate, the shame, they bring to us all

But still, a mother's love for her child never dies,
No matter how hard she tries
She replies, yes my child is a thief, murderer,
Crack head, drug addict,
Thug, prostitute, stripper, instigator,
Liar, cheater, manipulator,
A woman and a man beater
People judge what they see
And assume what they don't see
And what you don't see is the rhythm of our heartbeats

Just because my child has flaws and all
Makes me love them even the more
God has given me this child, you see, to make sure
That I love them unconditionally

Pain Is The Name of The Game

A mother's love for her child will never cease, you see
In the midst of all the grief my child has grown
More than just statistically

The young man or young girl
You thought they would never be
The lawyer, doctor, or debating in the presidency
I know you thought they would never make it
To the president's seat
So it would be wise
To take your mouth off of someone else's child
Open up the blinds, take a seat, and look in the mirror
At self-hate in thine own eyes
For a mother's love will never die,
No matter how hard she tries

It has no boundaries on how far it can go,
It's deeper than anyone can imagine,
Even deeper than your soul

A mother's love for her child never dies, it's a fact
She will give you her life
And defend you until hell comes back
So if you've ever wondered how you came to be,
It's because a mother's love stretches so far,
Further than your eyes can see

Nashya M. Williams

Jeremiah's Ballad

Before you were even thought of,
I believed I had no purpose
Chasing my hopes and dreams but still I had no motives
Meeting and running after pastors, ministers,
Bishops, and prophets
Hoping for a direct word from the Lord,
The answers to my questions

Praying night and day, attending every church service
Holding hands at altar calls,
Participating in corporate prayers,
But still no answers to my questions

Before you were even thought of,
I believed I had no purpose
Chasing my hopes and dreams but still I had no motives

Keeping myself busy, so I don't have the time to think,
They say an idle mind is the devil's playground,
True indeed,
That is the case
Suicidal thoughts were the name of my mind game,
My death bed was the goal
The devil was waiting to gain

No one loves me, no one cares, death is the only option,
So let me get prepared
Okay God, here I am, I'm ready to go,
And I'm ready to die
"I can't Shya, I just can't"
Were the words He pronounced

Pain Is The Name of The Game

Before you were even thought of,
I believed I had no purpose
Chasing my hopes and dreams but still I had no motives
I said then make this stop, make this go away,
The pain and suffering I can no longer sway
He quoted before I laid
"You're pregnant"
I denied
He replied, "Yes you are, you're pregnant with a boy"
No God, that's a lie

Now before I go on, let's be mindful
God is a man who keeps His promise
Numbers 23:19, that's what His word says
Then I synced in harmony with a man I lusted after,
February 22, 2013 was the date of revelation
I was upset, humiliated, stressed, and confused,
God I wanted to be married,
Before I spread this good news

Now I'm so subdued, what do I do?
Spoke with the father
And "abortion" was the only word he knew
After weeks of depression, I came to my senses
I commanded my flesh and spirit under subjection
God you've blessed me with this child,
He's not a mistake,
Now I'm praying for directions,
Please don't take him away

I then told the father no abortion will take place,
God will see fit for this child to be taken care of
With or without you and that is it
October 12, 2013 is a date I will never forget

Nashya M. Williams

Twelve hours of labor,
The discomfort was all so worth it
Disconnected from my womb,
The room was a complete silence,
Then out of nowhere I heard your little cries,
The tears started falling

That day we met, you looked at me
And I was still crying
Your eyes said to me, "Hi Mom, I'm Jeremiah"
Now you're here, I'm overjoyed that I finally had you
I will not lie, my prayer was that
God bless me with a child
Before I interacted with a man who gave me one of
God's most precious angels,
Because it could have been the other way,
With my medical record saying she died from AIDS

Before you were even thought of,
I believed I had no purpose
Chasing my hopes and dreams,
But still I had no motives
I've promised you in the womb,
I've even told you eye to eye,
Now I'm writing this ballad, so you know it's not a lie

I will not allow anyone to disappoint you
If I can help it,
But if it seems to happen, just know that I am here
To help you break it
You're my son, my heart, and my seed
I never knew just how much your presence was needed

Pain Is The Name of The Game

God gave me this revelation
The same year you were born
"Your son is the key to unlock every door"

Before you were even thought of,
I believed I had no purpose
Chasing my hopes and dreams but still I had no motives
I thank you for opening my doors
And making me a better person,
Our foundation will stand strong, because God is in it
Now that you are here, I've found my purpose,
Continuously chasing my hopes and dreams,
Because of you, I am now successful

Nashya M. Williams

Authentic

When it's at its full potential,
Original length or original ingredients
Authentic lies within its roots;
It's undefined, unrefined, and legitimized
The original state of being is when
It's the healthiest, strongest,
And most tasteful
Whether from the ground up or molded in your hands
You can't take away its original bland

Natural is more of the term to use;
It's the purest of purity
You can't take away its originality
Like people of you and I,
Whether we are people of color, individually

See we laugh at one another because we are different
Short, tall, big, or small
We all have our own personality
Many piercings and tattoos
Make you different to look at
Kinky hair, silky hair, curly hair, short hair
Long hair, colorful hair, spiky hair, no hair

See the origin of our uniqueness
Makes us different in our own way
No one can duplicate your way,
Not even on a sunny day
Many can imitate you if they may,
But to take from your origin is not the way
It would be like picking a peach from the tree,
Slicing and placing it into a frying pan

Pain Is The Name of The Game

Once it is overcooked,
It takes away from its authenticity
It has a different texture and taste from its original state
Many people you see you may not like,
But with respect comes dignity
Their originality doesn't have to be to your liking

So don't take away from their character
Their authenticity is what makes them the person
They have found themselves to be

Authentic

Acknowledgments

This book was very challenging to me. I dealt with the opinions of others and I felt as though I was making a mistake. I then began to have writers' block for months at a time. Once I began to share my experiences with others and began to read my poems from this book, the reaction I received was very different. I started to understand this book will help others as it was intended to do. It was at that time I gained more courage, confidence, and became passionate about the material I was putting out.

I often refer to Mary J. Blige, also known as the "Queen of Hip Hop and Soul". Her music is very relatable; people gravitate to what they can relate to. The same with "Pain Is The Name of The Game".

I want to thank you as a reader for taking the time to read my book. I hope you will get what it is that you need to see pain, but also begin to heal from the pain.

I would like to thank my family, friends, and mentors who have helped me to understand I am who I am, I will be who I will be, and let the rest take care of itself.

It's time for you to start your journey to healing.

Love you much!

Nashya M. Williams

Pain Is The Name of The Game

Nashya M. Williams

About the Author

Often told to "stay in a child's place", Author Nashya M. Williams was forced to shield her emotions when communicating with others, especially the adults in her life she so desperately wanted to connect with. This indirect, yet detrimental form of emotional bondage inspired a daily practice of diary-style writing, which developed into poetry at age 13.

Through personal reflections, Nashya learned how to cope with her pain in order to endure the many uncontrollable circumstances that life would throw her way. As a dedicated single mother and hard worker, Nashya's ultimate goal is to share the experiences and feelings that she suppressed for years, no longer hiding or being ashamed of her true identity.

Pain Is The Name of The Game

www.ingramcontent.com/pod-product-compliance
Lightning Source LLC
Chambersburg PA
CBHW020429010526
44118CB00010B/494